ENJOYING BLISSFUL LIVING

ENJOYING BLISSFUL LIVING

Dr. Bindya HSB Singh

GYAN

ISBN : 978-81-212-1237-3

Price : ₹ 90

First Published, 2015

Published by

Gyan Publishing House
23, Main Ansari Road, Darya Ganj,
New Delhi-110002
Ph. : 23282060, 23261060,
E-mail: books@gyanbooks.com

Laser Typesetting: Sanya Computers, Delhi,
Printed at: G. Print Process, Delhi

Cataloging in Publication Data—DK

Courtesy: D.K. Agencies (P) Ltd. <docinfo@dkagencies.com>

BHS, *Dr.,* **author.**
Enjoying blissful living / Dr. BHS.
pages cm
ISBN 9788121212373

1. Happiness. 2. Self-culture. I. Title.

DDC 158 23

Contents

Introduction

Enjoying life and living in bliss is everyone's birthright!

When peace, joy and harmony synchronise within us, we start living in bliss.

Man's journey on earth has two essential missions: First to enjoy life, and then to experience bliss.

That sounds like heaven, but we are here on Earth! Is it indeed possible to have a life full of enjoyment and bliss, irrespective of circumstances? Trust me, the answer is yes. And you do not want to miss it!

Many will say or think, "But you do not know how many problems I have to face. Again I will say, "I know, I have them too, probably just like you do!" But problems have nothing to do with enjoying life or experiencing bliss!

My father used to say, *a problem is not the problem; not finding a solution is the problem.* Interestingly, my research of twenty-seven years as a physician, and scientist reinforced this completely. I always knew that my father was right!

However, something happened one day—and a deep knowing, an internal wisdom emerged. In a flash, in fraction of a second, I experienced the realisation that no amount of problems can deter; nor are their solutions required, for experiencing enjoyment or bliss.

If you are ready for that realisation and a perpetual state of happiness, read on.......otherwise, put the book down, and start thinking about your problems!

In any case, wish you all the best!

Appeal to Readers

To enjoy life and live in bliss, experiencing a simple understanding and realisation is required.

To understand well, the less said, the better. To realise, read slowly and repeat. To experience, practice patiently.

Sometimes silence can teach us more truth than words!

Appeal to Readers

To enjoy life and live in bliss, experiencing a simple understanding and realisation is required.

To understand well, the less said, the better. To realise, read slowly and repeat. To experience, practice patiently.

Sometimes silence can teach us more truth than words!

1 Why There is No Bliss?

So what went wrong? If we are all born with the birthright of living in bliss, how come everyone is not beaming and exuding with joy?!

Simple question, simple answer; because we think too much! Most of us will ponder then, "But I will become dumb if I do not think!" and I will have to say, "No, you will become wise...and blissful!!" This is the only realisation that one needs to have to start enjoying and living in bliss. And yet, man today will have so much difficulty accepting and practicing it; hence you are welcome to this book. Well, look at the bright side, it is not even a lengthy discourse has pictures and quotations!!

On a more serious note, one has to realise that the feeling of bliss and pure enjoyment comes from the core of our being. It is a deep sense of peace and joy laced with gleeful harmony. It is a *feeling*, experienced in the centre of our being, so do not look for it in your thoughts or head area. The brain is merely a problem solving and physical sense perceiving, external world driven, analysing and judging assessment centre. There is no possibility of finding any bliss in that zone.

However, man today is continuously living and experiencing life from his brain. He is constantly 'thinking', enduring a never ending stream of thoughts in his head and in the process always judging himself, his relationships, situations, circumstances. In that state of existence there is no potential of finding any peace or joy, let alone bliss! Bliss, to me, is a state where peace, joy, and harmony blend in perfect proportions and bring a smile to one's face for no reason.

So in essence, am I trying to tell you that if you *stop thinking*, you will start living in bliss? Well, that is the most important initial part to get you there. And the only other aspect you need to be ready to accept, is to recognise that you are *part of a bigger whole.* If you don't accept the second request, you might transiently experience peace, but it will not last. And you will miss out on the most beautiful feeling of living in continuous bliss.

Let us look at the whole picture factually, and this might help us realise the second aspect mentioned in the above paragraph, "*being part of a bigger whole*". The universe is speculated to have existed for billions of years. While Earth and life on it have existed for millions of years, the oldest records of human existence as a fully developed, modern-behaviour man (*Homo sapiens*), have dated from 150,000 to 200,000 years ago. Historians suggest that older hominids (*human-like creatures that stood upright*) may have prevailed approximately 1.8 million years ago.

This is the time scale for humans like us to consider. The spatial orientation is also mind boggling...the Earth is a mere speck in the universe, considering it is speculated to be 93 million miles from the sun and 165 quadrillion miles from the dark hole of the Milky Way. It, itself, is only about 8000 miles in diameter! Put in perspective of the universe, which is thought to be about 80 octillion miles (80×10^{27}), each of us probably appears like a molecule of water in a vast spread of ocean!

Now please do not start thinking about the above details. Just picture yourself in relation to the universe, and you will feel a sense of existence in a time-space expanse. It should be easy thereafter to see that you are indeed a part of a big picture. You might even start wondering, like Albert Einstein did, "By whom/what and how was the Universe created?" Good, that means you are realising a power greater than your own that has been sustaining the universe, after it created it, for billions/millions of years!

Even if the creation of the universe were a random act, there must have been energies involved in the process. It had to be a very large and powerful energy or power source to have created the Universe. And that power must have created you as well! Wow, you are so connected to everything that there is!!

Again, you might feel very harmonious with your surroundings suddenly. If not, it is coming...

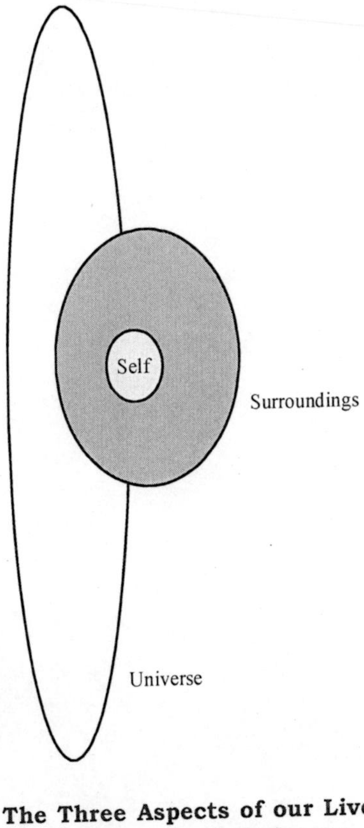

Fig. 1.1 The Three Aspects of our Lives: Self, Surroundings and Universe.

2 Problem and Solution

When a baby is born, nature intends it to start having fun right away! Otherwise it cries...sometimes so loudly that we want to run away!

Being a Neonatologist and Pediatrician, I realised (during a presentation and practice thereafter) that all babies intuitively know the road to mama's kitchen. And the baby is so set on having fun with food right after birth, although it is limited in its locomotive capabilities. It will snail its way to the breast of the mother, shortly after birth, even if, it is placed on the abdomen of the mother. What seems amazing is that the mother starts having natural breast milk production as soon as the newborn baby starts crying!! Wow, nature left nothing to chance!!

But as that little child grown up, he invests his interest in all kinds of unnatural needs and desires and an artificial world around him, which keep demanding more and more attention. Soon these so called unnatural inventions become essentials. Amazingly, the natural enjoyment goes flying out of his life to be replaced with a long list of demands, to the point that he forgets what it is to have simple joys in life.

Here is what has happened: Man's creation has started becoming his problem. The list of problems has grown so long that man has become buried in the list and lost his connections with nature, which created him to begin with. Man has come to know all the details of an atom and universe, but has forgotten who he himself is!

That is the tragedy, the problem with the problem, leading to the end of true enjoyment, and the beginning of pleasure era. The end of simplicity and starting point of complexity. The search for answers, to the complicated questions—which is his own creation. The quest for peace despite a large army and types of arms to maintain law, order and peace! The problem of needing safety after creating all kinds of safety gadgets! The desire for unconditional love in the midst of exploding lust! The need to find an honest friend in the ocean of millions of faces of electronic acquaintances! Can someone please help the poor little rich man!!

So is there a solution to the problem? If yes, is it easily available and applicable, and most importantly: Is it FREE?!

Now here is the good news: the solution is easily available, applicable, and completely free. And the best part is that it is within each human, just like the DNA in each cell, so there is no need to go chasing anything outside of us. No, not even our tails!

How can something as profound as a life full of enjoyment and bliss be so easy? Well, it is, but it is difficult to understand because our minds have become very complicated and have lost the simplicity to comprehend it and apply it.

So we need to make the solution a little complicated to make the mind in its current state able to understand it. And the simplest complicated way of looking at it involves three steps.

How do I know that these three steps will get us to bliss? Spent a lifetime searching and handled a truckload of unnecessary hurt along the way! Trust me, I was more lost than Lord Buddha, living a sensitive and compassionate life like Lord Jesus and always trying to seek righteous action like Lord Krishna!! And yet, had to face major emotional hurt due to relationships, circumstances and life situations....until the realisation dawned on me as the internal wisdom emerged.

So unless you want to go through half a century of searching and battling deadly evils along the way, listen up. Here is my simple realisation, for which you might have paid by now (if you cannot afford, ask for a refund!). Three steps to Bliss.....

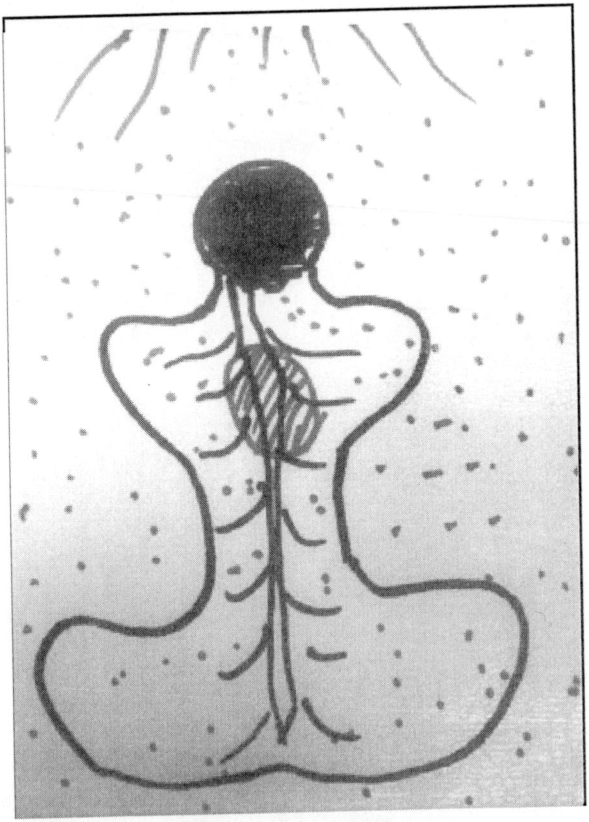

Fig. 2.1. Simplified Drawing for Conceptual Understanding of the Self: Body, Mind, and Soul Energies. Influencing the Self are Surrounding and Universal Energies.

3 Step One

The First Step is: Self-realisation

Hmm, what do I mean, everyone knows himself or herself? Yes, that is what we think, but what we know is a very tiny part of self. Eerie because when we know ourselves in totality, our jaws will drop and our smiles will extend from ear to ear with star like twinkle in our eyes! No, I am not talking about a Harry Potter movie, it is about You!

Ok, you probably think I am stretching this a bit much. But believe me when I say that this is the *sine qua non* for getting anywhere close to *bliss.* Someone put it very well: Realisation is finding the "Real I." And what is the "Real I"?

Look at yourself in the mirror from head to toe. See the physical body? Don't start fixing your hair or clothes now; none of that matters for feeling blissful! That physical body is merely the container of the "Real I." The body cannot do or feel anything unless another structure perceives it. Huh?! Yes, it is the mind, which registers all sensations and gives all kind of commands to the physical body to carry out action. The physical body is just a puppet, kept in shape and dressed like a toy or doll! *The physical body is not the "Real I."*

All right, now this mind guy seems very important—right? Kind of, so let us learn about it some more. Although the main seat of the mind is in the brain, the head area, it has connections all over the body through nerves. It also affects the physical body in other ways such as by releasing chemicals which are released in the blood and circulated to the entire body.

It appears that this mind dude is like some kind of mafia don! Almost, and it can be equally destructive. *But we can also get a lot of good out of our mind if we can conquer it, since it controls so much.* So what is the good part and what is the concerning part of mind? What part can control which part? In essence, how can we control the mind?

To conceptually understand the mind, put out your hand in front of you with the fingers spread out in a manner that the thumb points upwards and the little finger points down (Fig. 3.1).

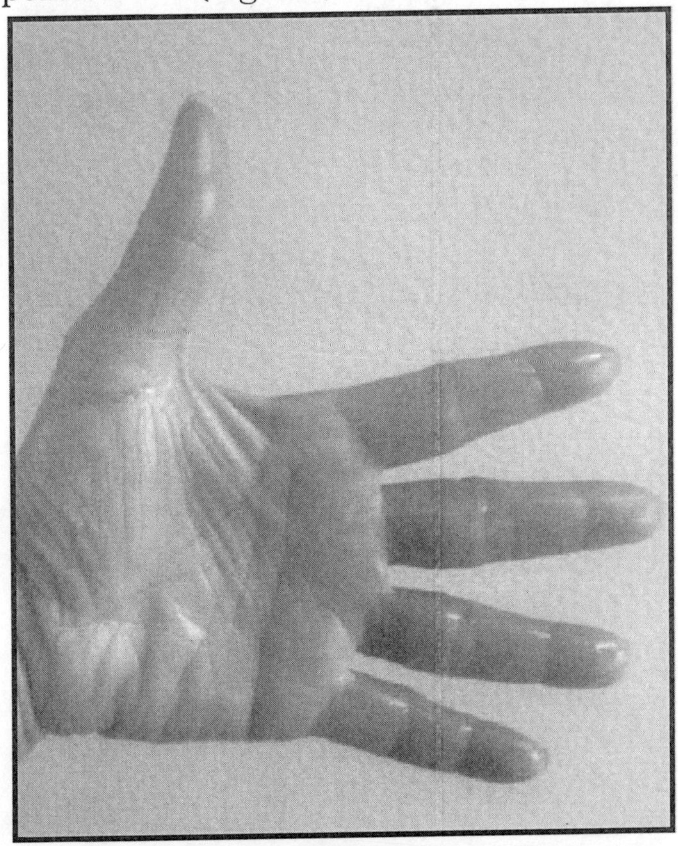

Fig. 3.1. Understanding Your Mind with the Hand and Fingers.

So the outstretched hand is like your mind and it's five functional aspects.

The little finger is the subconscious mind, which manifests as dreams when you are sleeping.

The ring finger is the observational mind that will look, hear, or sense surroundings without any thoughts. It simply observes and is oriented towards helping us navigate the physical world.

The middle finger (oh no! the bad sign one!) is the emotional mind. Seven basic emotions reside in our emotional mind according to psychologists: fear, anger, sadness, joy, disgust, acceptance, and surprise. Only two of these are positive: joy and acceptance. That combination, i.e., emotion of joy and acceptance put together, becomes love. So yes, it can be a beautiful part of the mind to be in, but the other five emotions can wreak havoc. These other negative emotions are often active when a part of the emotional mind, the ego, is predominant. When this part of the mind is hyperactive, it has recurring thoughts pertaining to "I" and "me." It is the part of the mind that creates a separate identity of itself, and like a two years old with terrible temper, it is always capable of throwing tantrums. It comes packaged with a gang of vices: greed, judgment, lust, anger, and pride. Acting out of the ego, one develops negative traits such as deceit, conceit, laziness, jealousy, and hate. It keeps feeling threatened and acts out by having recurring thoughts about an "*all-consuming perceived self-identity*" which is so overwhelming that the rest of us get completely ignored. It keeps us wrapped up in the past recollections and future apprehensions without any regards to the present moment. This is where our distress starts. Like a broken record, the ego repeatedly plays and replays thoughts such as: "I" am not good enough, "I" could not get that, he did that to "me", she said so and so about "me", they should not have treated "me" like this...imagine, if this is the only finger (the middle finger) operating in our lives, then we are scr...screaming! In it's hyperactive state, it can become a very distracting and deceiving part of the mind, distressing us unnecessarily!

The index finger is the intelligent part of the mind. Whether you are doing a puzzle, following a nice show, involved in a mathematic equation, solving a problem... this mind becomes active. By increasing concentration of this part of the mind, we are able to enhance our knowledge and gain information as well as utilise it in the future. Problem solving, analytic review, reading, comprehension, etc., required for intellectual and academic pursuits flourish in this part of the brain. It is a good mind to have operating, but not essential to use it continuously for survival. In fact, one should use it only when needed to get to the fun-filled enjoyment and blissful life!

The thumb is the most extraordinary finger—it points up if held as suggested in Fig. 3.1; it is strong and firm in its standing. It is the part of mind I like to refer to as super-consciousness. It is pure awareness of the rest of the minds, like a supervisor overseeing everything. This mind comes into operation when all other parts of the mind are on standstill. *The mind is completely quiet with no thought activity, and a person is alert and aware of everything around oneself.*

Take your time to be in that state for as long as possible. *A sudden sense of peace will be felt in the core of your being, in the heart region.* As you prolong this experience, you will feel complete peace internally and in absolute harmony with everything within and outside of you. *That energy field you have just touched is your soul! It is your life force, it is your true identity, the "Real I."*

I hope you are glad to meet yourself! Just by being fully alert in the present moment at any time you can access this life force. Keep handy reminders such as looking at your hand or chest region. Or watch your breath as if it is bringing nourishment to your soul. Or assign a word that you will give you an instant reminder of your true self, your soul, and use it when needed. If your quest is intense you can even frequently chant that word in the beginning of your practice of self-realisation.

Once you have encountered your soul, you will want to identify with it more than anything or anyone else. You will feel restless until you are consciously and continuously identified with it at all times. That one momentary experience will cause you to seek it more and more.

The realisation will dawn on you that you have been so used to having a plethora of unwanted thoughts in your head at all times. These thoughts can be as many as twenty to forty per minute! Most of them tend to be absolute nonsense and completely irrelevant to your current state of existence, pretty much just an "ego-trip." Since the ego is constantly feeling threatened, it is usually thinking negative thoughts in an attempt to "survive." So it constantly creates negative thoughts. You will also recognise that the unfortunate aspect of this state of mind is the creation of unpleasant feelings, such as anger, fear, sadness...this is so because each unpleasant thought comes with unpleasant feeling. What is worst is the concern that unpleasant feeling is associated with negative chemicals in the body that produce disease, distress, and aging!

However, with the realisation of your complete self, you will want to associate with the ever peaceful and joyous soul rather than the easily disturbed and constantly fluctuating mind. As you slow down in your thinking and start creating gaps in the stream of thoughts, complete internal peace will start becoming a reality for you.

You will start recognising that these peaceful times occur when you have pauses in your unnecessary thinking process. Soon you will find yourself in that state for longer and longer periods until you start living like that....all the time. You will feel fresh and relaxed as if you are a newly born baby. And yet, your alert consciousness, intelligence, and memory will be crystal clear and sharp.

No words, no description can be assigned to that wonderful experience, that realisation...and it gets better...

Stay with this step for a few days before you proceed to the next step (re-read and practice). The deeper and longer you are able to stay in this state of peace and joyous soul-consciousness, the more successful you will be in the next step.

4 Step Two

Ok, now that you know yourself, what's next? If I know myself and can keep myself strong, feel the peace within, why bother with more? Lesson complete, time for wrap up? No. You are going to come right back to read more as you fall flat on your face again. And when you fall, it will hurt. Don't do it. *Be fully alert, armoured, and attached to the right forces.*

Aha, got your attention because you are reading on! Well the second step is given away in the previous statement: Be fully alert, *armoured*, and attached to the right forces. You see, just like a soldier has to have the right ammunition to stay fighting and for protection needs a full armour to stay strong, we need to continuously replenish our resources with the right source of energy. What that means is to stay connected with the power house which will keep our energy source replenished!

We all know that there has to be an energy or power that has created and sustains the universe. None of us are responsible for bringing out the sun, moon, or the stars, so we know Man cannot run this Universe! However, another power does run this Universe. Let us call it the Universal Power or Supreme Power.

Also, if you look at yourself in the live state, you know that you are matter presenting as mass full of energy. How? Because *mass in motion is energy*, as described by the formula, $E=mc^2$. Right? Please do not argue about what the greatest brains of the world have already awarded the Nobel Prize to a genius (Albert Einstein) for!

Ok, so you are eventually energy and are surrounded by the energy of the Universe. How again? Because we are surrounded by life everywhere, which are like us, masses in motion, or energy.

For any energy to exist in continuum, it is connected with a power source. *In essence, we are all energy sources powered by the Universal Power.* So you can connect with that Universal Power which has ALL the powers in the universe. Well, why don't we then? Because you need to have the appropriately pronged plug to connect. And what it is that? *Only in the state of being soul-conscious can we connect with the Universal Power.*

As we have discussed in the previous chapter (Chapter 3: Step One), self-consciousness is a pure state of existence wherein you are completely living out of your soul. You are existing with complete purity of intent and attitude. That means you follow the one single rule of symbiosis that the universe demands: *the Golden Rule.*

What does this rule say? *Live with compassion.* Treat others as you want to be treated. Just that; nothing less, nothing more. The Golden Rule creates the connection to the powers of the entire universe. It is simply the *Golden Rule connection or The Law of the Universe.*

When we start living out of our souls, with a quiet and still state of mind, and reach out to the universe, we get connected with the Universal Power.

"Connect with the Universe" seems like a tall order, but it is truly very simple. Just start looking, hearing, or feeling nature starting from the Earth to the Sky. Look at the landscape and the skyline without any internal thoughts or dialogues—in complete silence. See yourself as an energy source connecting with the energy that runs the entire Universe.

How will it feel when you connect? You will feel a deepening of the soul's sense of peace and an emergence of deep joy connecting with the never-ending energy resource. There will be a feeling of a *pure, divine upsurge of unconditional love* and a feeling that you have no need to fear or worry about anything. A realisation that the power that created you, and of which you are a part, is always there to take care of you. It will provide you with complete acceptance, wisdom, and strength to do what is required—always.

The Universal Power will endow you with a realisation of being a part of the universe, a feeling of being *eternal and infinite!* You will feel as if the outer coverings of your body have dissolved and your core inner energy has extended to the entire universe.

Get out of the box you are in, the room, the building, and look at the horizon, and reach out to the universe...it has been waiting for your realisation and connection forever!!

Fig 4.1. Horizon and Feel the Energy of the Universe Reaching you from Infinity.

5 Step Three

Phew, down to the last step! Step Three is fortunately the easiest, and yet, the trickiest one to get right. Again, look at the statement: Be fully alert, armoured, and *attached to the right forces*.

With steps one and two under our belts, we should be feeling on top of the world! Maybe even literally! And yet, we may lose some of the positive energy as we start interacting with beings that are not soul-conscious. We all know those acquaintances, relatives, colleagues who make us uncomfortable. We may *perceive* them as annoying and sometimes even hurtful although they *should have no access to the remote controls of our mind by now.*

But boy, some of our relationships can take our attention away from our true focus and waste our energy! And the other concern is also worthy of consideration: What if they break and make us break the Golden Rule? What if their company brings out the worst in us by changing our outlook from soul back to the mind or body? Oh no, that will affect our Steps One and Two, which is to be in line with our true self, the "Real I" and stay connected with the Universal Power. We are bound to drop down from the coveted, elated divine peace and joyous state back to a life of distress! Hmm, dilemma!!

In my childhood I had learnt two very important lessons:

"You will eventually become the company you keep."

and

"Even if you are wearing white clothes of purity, stepping into black dirt of conceit will tarnish your clothes."

Got it? Keep the company of those who are blissful if that is what you want...

Seek the company of those who have what you want...

Can't find too many peaceful and joyous human beings? Seek the companionship of *other* beings that are peaceful and joyous. Loving pets for example. Be in the company of nature, trees, plants, leaves, flowers, peaceful animals, comedy shows, uplifting books. Maybe you will find people in spiritual sites; church, temple, synagogues, mosques, who have it already.

Build your living environment with plants, pictures, etc., which reinforce the feeling of tranquility. And remember it is much better to be alone than with those who are mind controlling, egoistic, and disruptive individuals. At least until this practice of being in enjoyment and blissful living becomes a continuous, unshakable process for you.

Once you are in a peaceful place surrounded by peaceful beings, synchronise with your surroundings. In addition to the internal peace that you felt with Step One and the joy of connection with Step Two, now you will feel a deep sense of synchrony and harmony with your surroundings.

You will feel one with your environment, as if the coverings of body and mind have melted away and you are one with your surroundings.

An experience will emerge wherein it will feel as if the energy within and without have become one...*it is a feeling of pure bliss.*

Soak in that bliss of peace, joy and harmony for as long as you can, for it is the most priceless feeling one can ever get...

Fig. 5.1. Each Plant and Tree is Trying to Tell you Something Silently...that they Love and Support You!

6 There You Go!

Once you have transcended all the three steps and tasted the bliss of life, nothing more needs to be learnt or said. You will know, all there is to know, from within, as if the DNA of wisdom that you were born with, has been turned on, or activated.

The reason that is possible is because each person is prepackaged with a complete blueprint of happiness, health, and success by the Universal Power, through the amazing works of nature. By keeping the connections of the Universal Power and synchrony with the environment, we allow the manifestation of our intended life.

What if you have to be in the company of disruptive beings for some time? Put on a double dose of your armour!! Start revising, reminding, and revisiting Steps One and Two in their company until they or their company passes. Stay out of your emotional mind which is driven by the ego.

Remember that none of what they say or do is about you; it is about them. *"If someone has a problem, it is their problem"*.

Knowing that you have the complete acceptance, support, and strength of the Universal Power, no one will have the capacity to break your peace, joy or harmony. This is how you dissociate yourself from the intent, attitude, thoughts, words and acts of others. This is how you do not let a product of someone else's doing affect your peace.

On the other hand, despite what someone is saying or doing, you will suddenly feel compassion and empathy for them instead of anger! The Golden Rule will teach you to live like that. You will feel a heightened sense of forgiveness rather than fear. A sense of gratitude rather than grievance. Patience rather than panic. Enjoyment rather than entanglement. Immense peace rather than irritation.

And yet, you will find the strength to maintain distance and send those who have harmed you love from far. If an action is required on your part, in that state of bliss you will know what is the right thing to do. A feeling of peace, joy and harmony, culminating in bliss, will abide in your being, irrespective of circumstance!

You will become cognisant of the five attributes of influence that any person can have: *Intent, Attitude, Thoughts, Words, and Actions*. All these can impact you as well as others. Those who become soul-conscious (either by nature or nurture) have purity in all those aspects. They never intentionally hurt others, and if they unknowingly do, are quick to seek forgiveness.

Eventually those who are struggling to find bliss will start seeking what you have been seeking as they sense your bliss. You can guide them from a distance, but do not get entangled in their lives or take on their problems because everyone must undertake his own journey!

You should not take up their burdens or negative energy, as you will lose your ascend. And only a person can transcend his own mind to find his soul and its universal connections. Sometimes challenges are given by the Universal Power to people to find a higher way of living. Hence, coming in the way of an individual's learning can be counter productive.

However, it might be that another person is at the end of their rope and desperately needs help sooner than later. So try and send them wisdom and love from far by giving them the information that has helped you. This may be in the form of notes, words, books, or electronic media (Videos, Audios, TV, Internet), healers in spiritual or medical field.

Remember the saying:

"Teach a man how to catch his fish rather than feed him every day."

Similarly, you cannot find a person's bliss for them; you can only show them the path. A simple three-step path, that you have hopefully mastered by now! And I sincerely pray that you will soon be blissful at all times, smiling irrespective of circumstances or company!

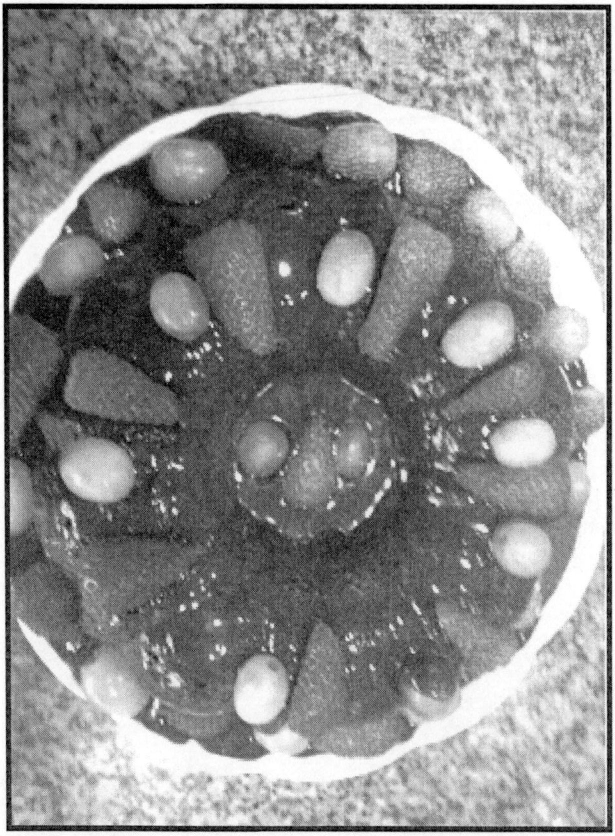

Fig. 6.1. Start Enjoying whatever you do. Simply Live through Soul. Live with Peace with Self, Joy with Supreme, and Harmony with Surroundings.

7 Staying There

All right, so we got it once and then again, but how do we stay in that state all the time? And why is it so difficult?

To answer the second question first, we need to understand the human bias. We have been programmed during our growing up process to use our minds excessively. Some parts of the mind are good to use at the right time, but unfortunately, some are more harmful. The more harmful mind I am referring to is the ego-mind, as we have discussed in previous chapters. This part of the mind gets more activated, more if we have failed to receive unconditional love in life. *Additionally, if we have been shown hate, dejection, or a lack of acceptance repeatedly, either in severe intensity or for a prolonged period of time, our egos perceive a threat to the mind made pseudo "self-image."* The false "self-image" can feel so threatened that it starts fighting for survival. In such a situation, the ego-mind becomes dysfunctional and overwhelmingly overactive to the point that it continuously generates thoughts pertaining to its survival. In that unfortunate state of mind, the compelling and recurrent thoughts overshadow all else, and the *mind starts overruling the soul.*

Just like the steam from boiling water can fog the window and cover the real scene, the overactive, burning ego-mind can overtake all other functions of the person. The result is that the disturbances created by the ever-thinking mind bury the peaceful soul. But in one instance of realising this paradigm and of making the switch from mind to soul (as shown in Chapters 3-5, Steps One to Three), we start our journey back to being blissful.

When the journey in a self realised state begins, enjoyment abounds! The simplest functions of life: eating, sleeping will start becoming so much fun. You will start enjoying whatever you eat or will seek good tasting and healthy food with ease. Your sleep will be deep and peaceful and you will feel extremely fresh in the morning. With the basics taken care of, you will want to be active during the day and without needing to think, will know what to do!

Now how do we stay there all the time? There are three possible ways. First, just let it happen. Yes, it will happen because you have gotten a glimpse of the most priceless feeling and you will seek it again and again until eventually you rest there by default at all times!

Second, place reminders around yourself, such as on your bathroom mirror, refrigerator door, desk, car, etc. This may be in the form of a symbol or a statement or a phrase. For example, in my initial stages of awakening, I placed the following card next to my computer screen: *Now, Faith, and Love.* I also placed shiny religious symbols of different faiths, live plants, toys, etc., at my desk and living area to be constantly reminded of my soul and Supreme connections.

Third, connect the feeling of bliss to a continuous activity of life. Breathing is one such activity. Reciting a blissful word mentally or visualising a peace inducing vision is another way. Or the best is to eventually completely be in the moment with an empty or blank mind, with no thoughts whatsoever. Whenever, I had absolutely nothing to do and just wanted to rest in peace, such as on a long journey, I would visualise the universe with the sun at its centre, recite a name from the scriptures, and feel the warmth of peace, joy, and harmony in each breath.

Take your pick or make your own design, but make sure you install a default blissful screensaver on your mental computer! And by whatever means, *stay there!! There is no other way to live!!!*

Fig. 7.1. Place Reminders Around Yourself, at Home and at Work, to Keep you Soul-conscious and Connected with Universe.

8 Finding Your Destiny

The life force on Earth has been created in its current state in the form of a pyramid. At the apex of the pyramid is man: you and me. We are the ones that the universe has granted with the complete know-how of *maintaining balance* even when we make changes. And in that framework, the powers of the universe have taken their own infinite energy and made sub-particles and packaged them in smaller units so that each may enjoy and live in bliss.

However, man, driven by his mind, sometimes gets too greedy and shrewd for his own good. This again is driven by his egoistic needs of self-gratification, often in a perverted sense. In that state the ego-driven mind neglects how much hurt and disrespect it shows towards others in quest for his personal desires. Unfortunately, in this insanity, a being drags another innocent person into hellish deeds of which we all eventually have to bear consequences.

But then the universe places checks and balances of its own accord, and man has to suffer for his inappropriate acts. Therein, we walk the path of deviation from our original purpose to enjoy life and live in bliss.

In essence, our original intent was to enjoy life in a blissful state. That is why our soul energy, which is a part of the universal energy, undertook a body to experience the world. To operate the body, the soul needed a mind, like the gears are needed by the driver to operate the car. The driver had an internal GPS to know where and how to go, but lo and behold, the cruise control of the car took over the driver! Cars (the body) started going out of control and hitting other cars; therefore, traffic jams and accidents became rampant. "Might is right" ruled, and chaos and disharmony prevailed. Man went from peace to panic, joy to distress, harmony to distraught. Disease and misery rather than health and happiness became the rule.

In a balanced state of connected and soul-conscious existence, happiness, health, and success are natural. Here is how: In a soul conscious state the inner peace allows us to find our inner wisdom and make clear and concise plans. It is the same concept as driving and finding your way easily and quickly in a un-crowded road. Also if your car's GPS signals are activated appropriately you receive the guidance from a higher power to take the right turns to get where you need to. *Similarly when your mind is clutter free of unnecessary thoughts your deepest wisdom laced with universal insight easily makes the right decisions.*

And the simplest switch man has to make is to go from a mind and body-conscious state of existence to a soul-conscious state of life. The purpose of life will become crystal clear in a fraction of a second...and our true and delightful destinies will find us...

Destiny to me is the choices we make with the chances we are given...

The choices that we are given are a result of our past choices...

But the present becomes the past of the future...

Hence each moment offers an opportunity to live an enlightened life and alter one's life direction to the best possible...

Fig. 8.1. As Long as You Live in Soul-consciousness, Harmonious with the Universe and Surroundings, a Delightful Destiny will Find You!

9 Effortless Success

Some questions I am often asked are the following: "Can one always be blissful and live successfully in this world?" and "Does one have to live an isolated life to be continuously blissful?"

Answer to first: Yes

Answer to second: No

You see, *the existence of enjoying a blissful life is a state of mind...or rather a state of "no-mind." Or to be more specific, a state of "no-ego-mind."* In that state, our intelligence, observation, alertness, consciousness, and soul-accessible, innate wisdom are all very easily accessible to us.

Considering that each "being" has complete wisdom within it's soul, we are always equipped with a set of integral wisdom wherever we are. Once the soul connects with the Universal Power, it receives motivation through unconditional love, and strength with harmony from its surroundings, and therefore each soul is able to activate it's dormant DNA of wisdom. The Universe promotes such a being to achieve whatever they want because it is the most effective way of maintaining the universe in a symbiotic state.

With continually applying the three steps, we are able to achieve the highly desirous state of complete bliss comprising of peace, joy, and harmony as follows:

- *Self-realisation: Peace*
- *Supreme Connection: Joy*
- *Synchrony of Surroundings: Harmony*

Medical science is discovering that most disease states in man are produced by extreme stress. Stress is a state of mind where continuous thoughts of worry and apprehension prevail. Accompanying those are release of nerve signals and chemicals in the body which start body destruction and the result is distress, and physical disease states. (Dis-ease: not at ease). So you see that by merely controlling your thoughts one can reverse such heavy burdens on our lives as distress and disease.

Sounds great! But how about success? Well, the three most important aspects of success are *wisdom* of what to do and how, *strength* to do what is needed when it is needed, and *motivation* to continue to persist. Here is how all of those are provided:

- *Self-realisation: Peace-Wisdom*
- *Supreme Connection: Joy-Love and Motivation*
- *Synchrony of Surroundings: Harmony-Strength*

Hence, the true self, once realised, brings with it the complete package of all the wisdom one needs to navigate life, including where to look for knowledge when needed.

With supreme connection and synchrony of surroundings, one is provided with unending strength and unconditional love that provides unfaltering motivation.

When it comes to making decisions about short term or long term plans, pertaining to self or family, one will have the clarity and intelligence to undertake the right course. Personal, social and professional life will become a source of joy rather than a burden. Even if we have to undertake routes or plans which turn out to be detours, one will enjoy the experience and be grateful for it.

The strength and wisdom will appear to be out of proportion to what you or others have thought you to be capable of in the past. And yet it will stand the test of time, proving you victorious in life.

When our lives are endowed with infinite and eternal wisdom, love, joy, motivation and strength, every moment becomes charming, enjoyable and successful. What else does one need?

Well now that you have what you need, it is time to rediscover your life filled with happiness, health and success. Start living with complete alertness in the present with a relaxed body and quiet mind, connected with your surroundings and the Universe.

Wish you the very best in Life!

Fig. 9.1. Only the Sun Eventually Controls Life on Earth, So Stop Worrying! After Every Sunset there is Sunrise!

But truly the sun never sets; it just exists in another hemisphere!!

Just by being completely alert in the present with a relaxed body and quiet mind we encounter our soul.

When our entire being through soul-consciousness synchronises with all there is, we melt and become one with the Universe.

In that state of existence an enjoyable, blissful life journey begins!